4 Is the fingerprint the most unique human feature?

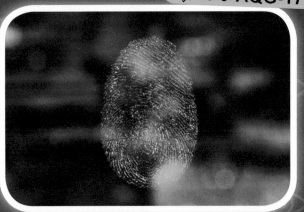

5 What does this machine do?

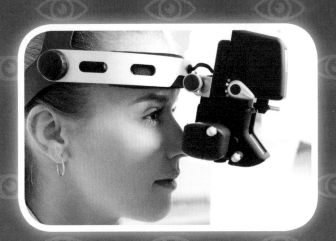

6 Why do honeybees have hairy eyes?

YOU CAN FIND THE ANSWERS TO THESE EYE-OPENING QUESTIONS AT THE BACK OF THE BOOK.

THE ULTIMATE GUIDE

EYES

SEE FOR YOURSELF!

THE ULTIMATE GUIDE TO EYES

Dorothea DePrisco

SEA GRASS

Brimming with creative inspiration, how-to projects, and useful information to enrich your everyday life, Quarto Knows is a favorite destination for those pursuing their interests and passions. Visit our site and dig deeper with our books into your area of interest: Quarto Creates, Quarto Cooks, Quarto Homes, Quarto Lives, Quarto Drives, Quarto Explores, Quarto Gifts, or Quarto Kids.

© 2017 Quarto Publishing Group USA Inc.
Text by Dorothea DePrisco

First Published in 2017 by Seagrass, an imprint of The Quarto Group.
6 Orchard Road, Suite 100, Lake Forest, CA 92630, USA.
T (949) 380-7510 F (949) 380-7575 **www.QuartoKnows.com**

Produced by Scout Books & Media Inc
President and Project Director Susan Knopf
Editorial Team Brittany Gialanella, Beth Adelman, Chelsea Burris
Index Arc Indexing, Inc.
Page Layout DKD&AD

Seagrass titles are also available at discount for retail, wholesale, promotional, and bulk purchase. For details, contact the Special Sales Manager by email at specialsales@quarto.com or by mail at The Quarto Group, Attn: Special Sales Manager, 401 Second Avenue North, Suite 310, Minneapolis, MN 55401 USA.

ISBN: 978-1-63322-376-9

Printed in China
10 9 8 7 6 5 4 3 2 1

TABLE OF CONTENTS

THE WIDE WORLD OF EYES

Our eyes give us one of our most important senses—vision. They help us pick out a good apple at the grocery store, watch a ball as we try to hit it with a bat, and see the moon in the sky.

WHAT YOU SEE

Eyelids
Upper and lower eyelids are folds of skin that cover and protect eyes when they are closed.

Eyelashes
Short, curved hairs grow around the eyelids to protect the eyes from dust.

Sclera
The white of the eye, this forms the outer layer of the eyeball.

Pupil
This round, dark center of the eye lets in light.

Tear Ducts
These are on the inside corners of the upper and lower eyelids. This is where tears drain from the eyes into the nose.

Iris
The colored part around the pupil helps the pupil open and close.

BEHIND THE SCENES

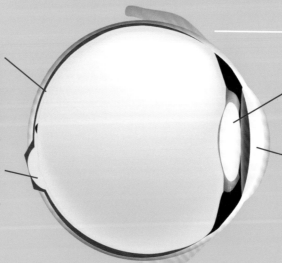

→ FRONT OF EYE

Retina
This membrane lines the eye and receives images formed by the lens. It changes them into signals that go to the brain.

Optic Nerve
This carries electrical impulses from the retina to the brain.

Lens
The lens focuses light onto the retina to create an image.

Cornea
This is a thick layer of cells that protects the eye and helps it focus.

MY EYES

You're made up of half of your mother's genes and half of your father's genes. (Genes carry information that is passed down from your parents to you.) When those genes combine, it's like a recipe with lots of ingredients. You inherit your eye color from your parents' genes, but you may not have the same color eyes as them.

PARENT 1	PARENT 2		Probable Color		
👁	+ 👁	=	75%	7%	19%
👁	+ 👁	=	50%	0%	50%
👁	+ 👁	=	50%	38%	12%
👁	+ 👁	=	0%	1%	99%
👁	+ 👁	=	0%	50%	50%
👁	+ 👁	=	0%	75%	25%

COLOR PALETTE

The pigment (called melanin) in your iris forms your eye color. The more melanin you have, the darker your eyes. The less you have, the lighter your eyes.

👁 The most common eye color is BROWN. About 55% of people around the world have brown eyes.

👁 About 8% of all people have HAZEL eyes. Their eye color may appear to shift from brown to green and back again.

👁 BLUE eyes occur in about 17% of all people. Some have light blue eyes, others have deep blue eyes.

👁 GREEN is the least common eye color. Only 2% of people have green eyes.

👁 Other colors and variations are much rarer. They include GRAY, SILVER, AMBER, and VIOLET.

1 + 1 = 2

Too much or too little melanin can result in two different color eyes. This occurs in some types of dogs, cats, horses, and other animals. People can have two different eye colors, as well. The scientific name for this is heterochromia. *Hetero* means "different" and *chromia* means "color."

ANIMAL
PEEPERS

Nearly all animals have eyes to help them find food and shelter. Some use visual cues, such as color and pattern, to recognize or attract mates. Eyesight also helps them spot and avoid predators.

FROGS

Frogs have big, bulging eyes on top of their heads, which helps them see anything that might creep up beside them. When they eat, they pull their eyes down into the roofs of their mouths (shown at right). This motion helps push food down their throats.

GECKOS

These nighttime hunters have big eyes that help them see color in the dark. This means they can find tiny insects to eat. Most geckos don't have eyelids, so they use their long tongues like windshield wipers to clean their eyes.

OWLS

Large eyes help owls see at night. Large pupils help them spot far-away prey. Instead of eyeballs, their eyes are long tubes attached to the back of the skull. The eyes don't move, so owls can turn their heads 270 degrees, or 3/4 of the way, to look around.

Leaf-tailed gecko

GOATS

Goats have unusual looking eyes. The pupils are horizontal rectangles. These special pupils give them a wide field of vision—they can see nearly 360 degrees around without turning their heads. This helps them spot predators and escape.

INVERTEBRATES

Invertebrates don't have a backbone or spine. Insects like butterflies and grasshoppers are invertebrates. So are spiders, sea stars, sponges, worms, squid, and mussels. Most have compound eyes (made up of many eye parts), simple eyes (with just one lens), or both.

Jumping spiders hunt by pouncing on prey. They have four pairs of eyes that help them judge the distance they need to jump.

Dragonflies and damselflies have two large compound eyes with thousands of parts called ommatidium. These help them judge distances and detect motion. Three small simple eyes, just below the compound eyes, help them sense light, which may help them tell night from day.

The bright color of blue morpho butterflies is easily spotted in their rain forest home. Potential mates are attracted by the color.

WHAT ANIMALS SEE

Night Vision Raccoons are nocturnal animals—they are active at night. Their eyes can focus and take in more light when it's dark.

What humans see

What birds see

Invisible Light Birds can see ultraviolet (UV) light, which is invisible to the human eye.

Heat pits

Thermal Vision Some snakes, such as this green tree python, use heat-sensing pits on their faces to "see" other living things and transmit visual information to their brains.

Blind spot

Blind Spot Horses have monocular vision—their eyes are on the sides of their heads. There is a blind spot—an area they can't see—in front of their faces.

What bees see

What humans see

Bee Bright Bees can't see all the colors people can see, but they can see UV light (invisible to the human eye). Flowers reflect UV light, providing a big target, known as a "honey guide," to help bees spot pollen.

Puffin' Up Puffer fish puff themselves up to look larger, to scare off anyone who may want to attack them.

Up Periscope! Orcas sometimes hold themselves upright and poke their heads above the water to check out their surroundings. This is called spyhopping.

Color Change Bigfin reef squid change color to hide, to warn off others, or when excited. Cells called chromatophores (*chromato* means "color" and *phore* means "bearer") carry color throughout the body.

Spot Alert The bright orange spots on a gila monster warn others off. They are a way of saying, "I'm poisonous, back off!"

Light It Up Fireflies communicate with visual light signals called bioluminescence. A chemical reaction in their bodies causes them to light up.

ANIMAL ANTICS

TOOLS FOR SURVIVAL

An adaptation is a change that makes it easier to live and thrive. Some animals have visual adaptations, which means their eyes and vision help them survive in their environments.

▲ A rabbit can spot a tasty treat with one eye and look out for a fox with the other.

BINOCULAR VISION

Animals with binocular vision have eyes at the front of the head that face forward. (*Bini* means "two together.") The vision in one eye overlaps with the vision in the other, as they work together to focus on a single object. Animals with binocular vision, including birds, humans and other primates, can judge distance.

◀ *Binocular vision helps people catch, grasp, and move around.*

MONOCULAR VISION

Some animals have monocular vision. (*Mono* means "one" and *ocular* comes from *oculus*, which means "eye.") Their eyes are on opposite sides of their heads, and each eye works independently. That means one eye can look left and the other right, taking in different images, but they can't judge distances well. Prey animals usually have monocular vision.

▲ *Grey crowned cranes have eyes on the side that can also face forward.*

FRONT AND SIDES

Chameleons have monocular vision. Their eyes can rotate nearly 180 degrees in their sockets, so chameleons can see nearly all around their bodies. And they can switch to binocular vision, making both eyes work together to see a single object. This forward focus helps them while hunting.

ABOVE-THE-WATER VISION

Crocodiles are ambush predators—they wait for prey to come by and then strike. Their vision is better above the water than below, so they scan the shoreline for prey. They don't have to move their heads, because their eyes do all of the work.

UNDERWATER VISION

Hammerhead shark eyes are located at the ends of their very wide, T-shaped heads. This gives them a wide field of vision (the area that can be seen without moving the head), which helps them spot prey and avoid predators.

▲ *Tyrannosaurus rex was a fierce dinosaur with excellent vision. It could see things 10 times farther away than humans can. It also had an excellent sense of smell, which helped it hunt at night.*

TRUE COLORS

How can we know what animals see? One thing scientists study is the number of color receptors, called cones, in eyes. Human eyes have three types of cones. Working together, our eyes and brains can perceive more than a million different colors. How many cones do other animals have to help them see colors?

OCTOPUS — 1 CONE

CAT — 2 CONES

CHIMPANZEE — 3 CONES

BUTTERFLY — 4 CONES

PIGEON — 5 CONES

MANTIS SHRIMP — 12 CONES

When it comes to eyes, some animals have a lot of them. Others have them in unusual places. And some have eyes that change location over time.

▼ Eye Relocation

When a halibut hatches, it has an eye on either side of its head. It swims upright. Over time, its body gets flatter. One eye moves over the top of the fish's head. Both eyes are then on the top its flat body, giving it the vision it needs for its adult form.

▲ Eyes on Top

Hermit crabs have compound eyes that sit on top of eye stalks. The eyestalks are up high and can move. This helps them see all around.

▼ No Eyes

The Texas blind salamander lives in water-filled dark caves. Over time, this creature stopped developing eyes because it did not need them. Two black spots on the face remain where eyes used to be.

Migrated eye

Eyespot

▶ Eyes on Arms

This sea star isn't waving; it's checking things out. Sea stars have tiny red eyes—one at the end of each arm. They can't see far, though—just a few feet around them.

▲ Two Eyes, Four Parts

Four-eyed fish can look up and down at the same time. Each pupil is divided in two. The top part can see above the water and looks for food. The lower part of the eye is below the water and keeps a lookout for predators.

▼ The Most Eyes

Scallops have eyes, and lots of them! The eyes are on the mantle (the outer edge of the body). Bay scallops have about 100 bright blue eyes. The eyes can recognize light and darkness, and spot food floating in the water nearby.

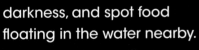

▼ Biggest Eyes for Its Size

Tarsiers have the largest eyes of any mammal relative to their size. Each eyeball is the size of the brain.

HELPERS

BUDDY, THE FIRST SEEING EYE DOG

Morris Frank (1908–1980) lost the sight in one eye when he was 6 and in the other at age 16. He was 19 when learned about Dorothy Eustis, an American living in Switzerland who was training German shepherds as guide dogs for veterans of World War I who had lost their eyesight. Morris wrote to Dorothy and asked her to train a dog for him. A year later, in 1928, he returned to the United States with his new guide dog, Buddy. Morris was a cofounder of The Seeing Eye in 1929. It is the oldest active guide dog training facility in the United States.

A guide dog helps its handler get around and keeps him or her safe. The handler directs the dog using commands such as "forward." If the roadway is clear, the dog proceeds. But what if a car turns in to a crosswalk? Guide dogs are taught "intelligent disobedience." This means they will disobey a command that would put the handler in danger.

HANDHELD DEVICES

A long white cane helps with independent travel. It also lets drivers and others know that the user is blind or visually impaired. It can be used with a talking GPS app on a smartphone.

OCTOBER
15

▲ White Cane Safety Day

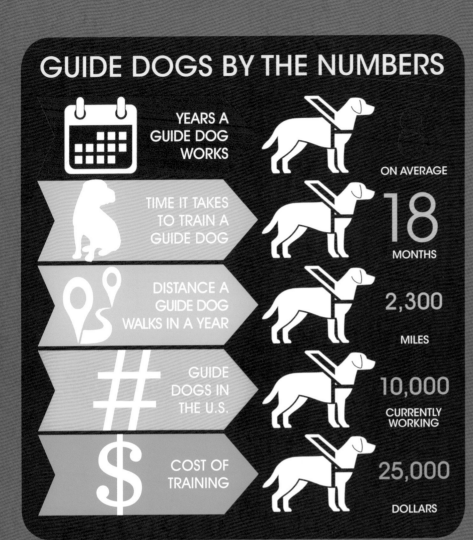

GUIDE DOGS BY THE NUMBERS

YEARS A GUIDE DOG WORKS		ON AVERAGE
TIME IT TAKES TO TRAIN A GUIDE DOG		**18** MONTHS
DISTANCE A GUIDE DOG WALKS IN A YEAR		**2,300** MILES
GUIDE DOGS IN THE U.S.		**10,000** CURRENTLY WORKING
COST OF TRAINING		**25,000** DOLLARS

Smart and Eager
Labrador retrievers, German shepherds, and golden retrievers are intelligent and have good personalities for service dog training.

LONG-DISTANCE HELP

A marathon is a race that covers just over 26 miles along a set route, often with tens of thousands of runners competing. How can a person with visual impairment follow the route and navigate the crowded race? Race organizers pair blind runners with volunteer guides—sighted runners who run at the same pace. The guide tells the runner when to turn, if they're approaching a big hill, and where other runners are on the course. The two runners may be connected by a string or rope.

PICTURE PERFECT

Your eyes are like a living camera. They send pictures of things you see to your brain. A camera stores pictures on a computer chip or film. Your brain processes—or figures out—what you are looking at in a fraction of a second.

HOW DOES THE HUMAN EYE WORK?

Light passes from an object through the lens of the eye. The iris dilates (gets bigger), making the pupil smaller. (The smaller the pupil, the less light can enter.) The lens focuses the light and sends it to the back of the eye. The picture is upside down. The retina, in the back of the eye, sends the picture as an electrical signal to the brain. The brain flips the picture right-side up.

SNAP!

What happens when a camera takes a picture, and how similar is it to how our eyes work? Here's a look at how eyes and cameras take pictures.

Eye

Iris

Pupil

Lens

Retina

Optic Nerve
to Brain

Which Way Is Up?

Why do our eyes see things upside down? Because the lens of the eye is convex, which means it's curved outward, like the back of a spoon. The visual part of our brains turns the image right-side up.

Try This at Home!

Hold a spoon up to your face with the back of the spoon facing you. Look at your reflection; it should be right-side up. Now turn the spoon so the front is facing you. Your reflection will be upside down.

▲ **Monkey See**

How fast can images travel from our eyes to our brains? A 2014 study showed that humans can process images in 13/1000 of a second. Macaque monkeys can process some images, such as faces, in 14/1000 of a second. Experts think that a macaque can recognize its own face in a mirror.

Camera

Lens

Aperture

Diaphragm

Sensor

COLOR *AND* VISION

VISIBLE LIGHT

Light is a kind of energy that travels in waves. The full spectrum, or range, of light includes visible light, which is the light humans can see. Invisible light falls at either end of the spectrum. Some animals can see light that humans cannot see. And invisible light is used in science and technology.

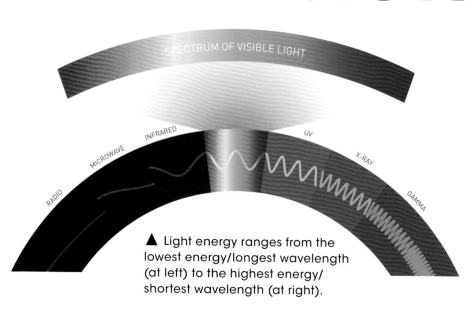

SPECTRUM OF VISIBLE LIGHT

RADIO
MICROWAVE
INFRARED
UV
X-RAY
GAMMA

▲ Light energy ranges from the lowest energy/longest wavelength (at left) to the highest energy/ shortest wavelength (at right).

HOW LIGHT BECOMES COLOR

The light we see travels in a straight line. It is colorless until it hits an object. Different colors of light travel at different speeds. When light changes direction, which is called refraction, the different colors traveling at different speeds can become visible. This is shown clearly in a glass prism. When sunlight is refracted by raindrops, a rainbow forms.

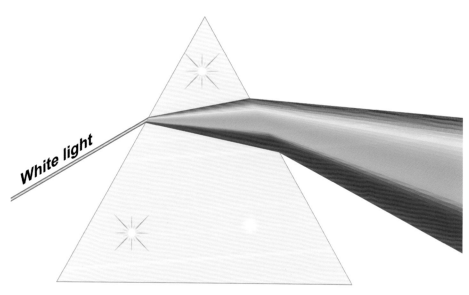

White light

ROY G. BIV

The colors in the visible light spectrum appear in a specific order. A common way to remember the order is ROY G. BIV, which is formed by the first letter of each color.

Red

Orange

Yellow

Green

Blue

Indigo

Violet

HOW WE SEE COLORS

The retinas in our eyes are lined with cells called rods and cones.

- The rods work in dim light. They don't help us see color, which is why we don't see color well in the dark. Nocturnal animals have many more rod cells than humans do.

- The cones work in brighter light. They help us see color. Our eyes have three types of cones: blue, green, and red. These are the colors they are most sensitive to, but each cone can detect a range of colors.

Cones send signals along the optic nerve to the brain. Through this eye-brain connection, humans can see more than a million colors.

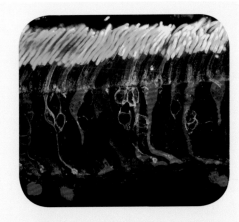

▲ Rods and cones in a human eye

▲ Cone cells

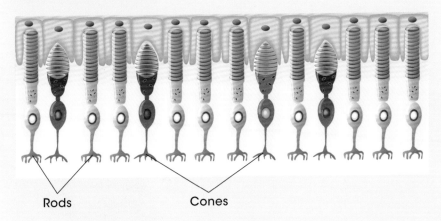

Rods   Cones

The human eye has more than 100 million rod cells and 6 million cone cells.

CRITTER COLORS

Some animals have fewer types of cone cells and can see fewer colors than humans. Dogs, cats, and squirrels are animals with just two types of cone cells. Some animals—such as great apes, kangaroos, and honeybees—have the same number as humans. And others, including butterflies and pigeons, have five types of cone cells.

SPOTLIGHTONEYES

Some animals have fully developed eyes that collect information on light, color, shape, motion, and depth. Others have simple eyespots that can sense only light. Here's a look at the evolution of eyes, and animals with eyes at different stages.

EVOLUTION OF THE EYE

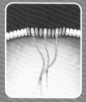

Eyespot
An eyespot is a group of cells that collect light. Animals with eyespots can see light but not where it is coming from.

Pigment eyecup
Eyes with holes or pits have light-sensitive cells. They collect the light and can sense which direction the light is coming from.

Simple pinhole eye
More developed eyes have deeper cups. These eyes can see light and where it is coming from. They can also sense shapes.

Primitive lensed eye
These eyes have lenses—a group of clear cells covering the opening of the eye. This allows clearer vision and keeps infections out of the eye.

Complex camera-type eye
A hard lens can focus the light. It is curved, which helps the eye focus near and far.

◄ **Planaria (flatworm)**

▼ **Abalone**

◄ **Nautilus**

▲ **Marine snail**

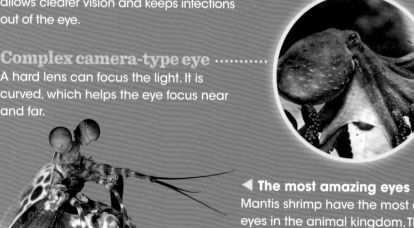

◄ **Octopus**

◄ **The most amazing eyes**
Mantis shrimp have the most complex and developed eyes in the animal kingdom. They have extraordinary sight, and they are able to see more colors than humans. Their eyes move independently and they can see all around.

BUILT-IN PROTECTORS

Blinking spreads tears across our eyes to keep them moist and clean. Our tear film is made up of water, salt, oil, and mucus. It protects our eyes from dirt and infection. These kinds of tears are called continuous tears. Reactive tears form when dust or sand get in our eyes—we react to things that irritate the eyes. Emotional tears form when we are upset or sad, and sometimes when we are very happy.

Baby Tears

Before they can speak, babies cry to communicate. They cry loudly, softly, and make high-pitched sounds, too. A parent starts to notice there are different cries for different things. For example, a high-pitched cry may mean, "I'm hungry!"

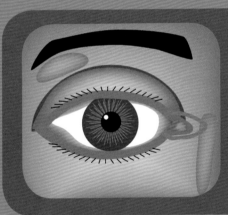

Where Do They Come From and Where Do They Go?

Tears form in glands over the eyes. They travel to the eyes in small tubelike vessels. Then they exit through two very small holes on your upper and lower lids. From there, they enter tear ducts and go down your throat or into your nose. When you shed a lot of tears, they also spill over your eyelashes and down your cheeks. Tear glands and ducts are shown in gray.

Lash-tastic

Eyelashes not only catch our tears, they help keep dust and dirt out of the eyes. And they can sense things like mosquitoes that are getting too close and blink or close automatically. Here are some animals with impressive eyelashes (top row) or body parts that protect the eyes in a similar way (bottom row).

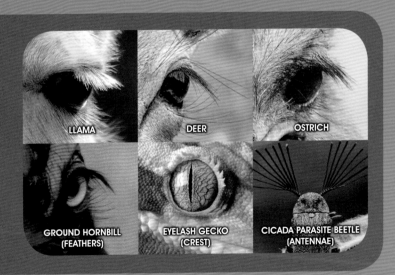

LLAMA

DEER

OSTRICH

GROUND HORNBILL (FEATHERS)

EYELASH GECKO (CREST)

CICADA PARASITE BEETLE (ANTENNAE)

EAT SMART

Did you know that the food you eat can help your eyes? There are foods that help prevent eye diseases and protect your eyes from infections. Here are some important foods to eat for better eye health.

Vitamin A ▶
Carrots, kale, spinach, milk, and egg yolks are foods that help your cornea (the thin layer at the front of your eyes). If you have dry eyes, they feel itchy and gritty. These foods help keep your eyes moist and comfortable.

Vitamin C ▶
Citrus fruits (especially kiwi fruit) and juices, green peppers, broccoli, and potatoes also help keep your cornea healthy.

◀ Vitamin E
Found in eggs, whole grains, vegetable oils, and sunflower seeds, vitamin E helps protect your eyes from disease.

◀ Fatty Acids
What do these foods have in common: coldwater fish (such as rainbow trout, salmon, and mackerel), sunflower oil, and corn oil? They help keep the retina healthy, and they power your brain, too.

Lutein ▶
Your body doesn't make lutein, so look for it in green veggies such as spinach, kale, broccoli, and Brussels sprouts. It protects your eyes from too much sun exposure.

Zinc ▶
To protect your eyes from disease, also look for foods that contain the mineral zinc. These include meat, poultry, fish, whole grains, and dairy products.

TAKE CARE

What you do can help your eyes, too. And there are some things, like rubbing your eyes, that are bad for them. Here are some key ways to protect your peepers.

▲ **Follow the 20-20-20 rule** when you're looking at a computer, tablet, or television screen. Every 20 minutes, take a break and look at something 20 feet away for 20 seconds.

▲ **Wear glasses** or contact lenses if you need them. We all deserve the best possible vision we can have.

▼ **Don't touch** or rub your eyes. That introduces dirt and germs, which can cause irritation and infections.

▼ **Wear protective gear** when playing sports, such as helmets with face guards, goggles, or eye shields.

▲ **Sunglasses** protect your eyes from the sun's damaging rays. Make sure you wear them at the pool and beach, and in the bright sun in the winter, too.

▲ **Go to sleep** on time. Getting enough sleep helps your eyes recover from the hard work they do when you're awake.

KEEP 'EM SAFE

GOODBYE, GERMS

Our hands pick up germs from all around. When we rub our eyes, they transfer germs on our hands to our eyes. This can cause an infection and hurt our vision. How can you fight germs?

 The most important step to protect your eyes is not to touch your face and eyes.

 The next important step is to wash your hands often. Use warm water and soap for at least 20 seconds.

 Not sharing is caring. Don't share towels, pillows, or washcloths with anyone. Germs live there and can be transferred from one person to another.

IT'S A SCIENCE!

In the science lab, chemicals or other dangerous materials may be used. Safety equipment to protect your eyes includes glasses or goggles and an eyewash fountain to flush your eyes in case of an accident.

▼ *Emergency eyewash station*

SUNGLASSES

Sunglasses and hats protect your eyes from the sun's glare on the beach, at the pool, or on the field.

FUN GLASSES

Sunglasses, also called shades, can match your style or mood.

SNOW SAFETY

Sunlight reflects off the snow, too, so be sure to wear sunglasses during winter activities. Special goggles designed for snowboarding and skiing protect your eyes from the cold and wind as well as sunlight and glare.

SIGHT SAVERS

Some inventions help people see more clearly. Others protect eyes from damage or injury. Here are just a few.

GOGGLES

Your eyes were not made to be under water. Goggles protect them when you swim in a pool or the ocean, keeping pool chemicals and salt water from hurting your eyes. They also help you see clearly under the water.

SUNGLASSES

Sunglasses keep your eyes safe from ultraviolet (UV) rays. UV rays are the rays from the sun that give you a sunburn. On the beach or in the snow, your eyes can get a kind of sunburn and become red, itchy, or swollen.

CONTACT LENSES

Contacts are little lenses for your eyes. They are very thin, soft, and clear. Contacts are made using a doctor's prescription, so they will correct vision in just the right way. Some contacts are worn only during the day, and some can be worn over a longer period of time. More than 25 million Americans ages 18 and up wear contacts.

PROFILE: Benjamin Franklin

Benjamin Franklin was one of the founders of the United States, and he helped draft the Declaration of Independence. He was also a printer and publisher, scientist, and inventor. He needed to wear eyeglasses and had two sets—one for reading close up and one for seeing far away. He was frustrated by frequently having to change which glasses he wore. He decided to invent glasses that would help him see both close up and far away. Called bifocals, these eyeglasses have split lenses. One half of the lens helps the wearer see close up and one half of the lens helps the wearer see far away.

Eyeglasses with bifocal lenses

Pros who keep their eyes safe

Chemists wear goggles to protect them from harmful fumes or splashes.

Athletes such as **snowboarders** and **skiers** wear goggles that have a UV coating to protect their eyes from sunlight reflecting off the snow.

Construction workers and **carpenters** wear safety glasses to protect their eyes from flying debris such as dust and bits of wood.

Dentists wear goggles and a mask to keep bacteria and germs away. They protect their eyes from splashes and dental material.

Welders wear face shields to protect their eyes and faces from the heat and UV light. They also wear safety glasses so their eyes are protected when they lift their shields.

Some **basketball players** wear eye shields to protect their eyes from flying balls and other possible injuries.

Named Dee-O-Gee, this golden retriever puppy is training to be a **guide dog**. Sporting impact-resistant dog goggles to protect her eyes, she is ready for a walk with her mentor, NASA engineer Evan J. Horowitz.

WHAT HAPPENS DURING AN EYE EXAM?

Here are some tools and tests eye doctors, called ophthalmologists, use to check your eyes and vision.

Cover Test
Your eyes work together as a team. This test helps the doctor make sure each one is doing a good job.

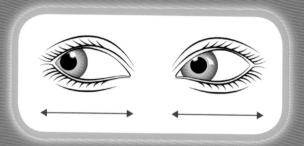

Eye Movement Test
Your doctor will ask you to follow a light or a finger from side to side without moving your head. This tests how well your eyes move together.

KNOW A PRO: OPHTHALMOLOGIST

An ophthalmologist is a medical doctor who helps people with their eyes and vision by diagnosing and treating problems. To become an ophthalmologist, a person needs to complete college and medical school, and then complete four years of special training.

Other people who may check your eyes or vision:

Pediatrician • Family Doctor • School Nurse • Optometrist

Slit Lamp

A bright light and a microscope help the doctor examine things near the front of your eye, including the eyelids, lashes, cornea, and iris.

Eye Pressure Test

A quick puff of air tests the pressure in your eyes. High pressure can be a sign of a problem called glaucoma.

Pupil Dilation

To get the best look into your eyes, the doctor may put eye drops in. The eye drops will make your pupils larger and this gives the doctor a better view all the way to the retina.

Color Vision Test

People who are color deficient cannot see red, green, and blue light the same way others can. For this test, you will look at patterns of circles with dots and shapes in many colors. If you see the hidden number inside the large circle, you are not color blind.

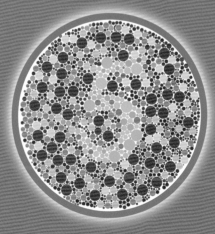

EYE CHARTS

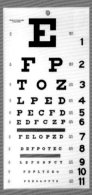

Snellen Chart This chart shows 11 rows of capital letters. The top row has a large E. The other rows get smaller and smaller. Your doctor will ask you to find the smallest line of letters you can see and ask you to read them.

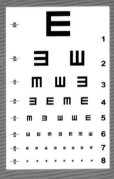

Tumbling E Chart This chart uses the same letter—an E—in different positions. If you're asked to read this chart, you'll indicate which way the E is facing–up, down, left, or right.

Animals/Objects Very young children may be asked to name animals, or point to other objects or pick out shapes such as circles or squares.

HAVING YOUR EYES EXAMINED FOR GLASSES

Normal vision is called 20/20, which means you can see clearly at 20 feet what most people can see at that distance. If the second number is lower, it means you have supersharp vision. If the second number is higher than 20, your vision is not as good and you may need eyeglasses.

PHOROPTER

Since each eye is different, this special machine tests each one individually. It contains different lenses for a patient to try while reading an eye chart. This shows which lens makes blurred vision supersharp and focused, so eyeglasses can be made with the right shape, curve, and thickness.

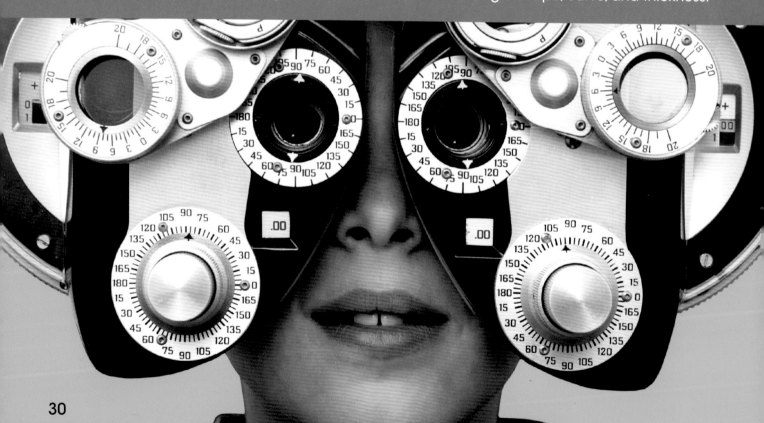

A doctor of optometry, also called an O.D., examines your eyes and diagnoses and treats problems with eye health and vision. An O.D. may prescribe and help fit you with eyeglasses, and can provide other vision aids and therapies. Training includes four years of college, and a degree from a college of optometry.

ON A CLEAR DAY

Some people have trouble seeing things nearby, but faraway objects look sharp and clear. That means they are farsighted. If objects nearby are in focus, but things far away look blurry, they are nearsighted. The right glasses can correct these conditions.

Nearsighted

Farsighted

Corrected

EAGLE-EYED . . . *OWL?*

How many eyelids do owls have? Three! The top eyelid closes when blinking. The bottom eyelid closes during sleep. The third eyelid, called a nictitating membrane, cleans and moistens the eye. It sweeps over the eye diagonally, like a windshield wiper.

◄ *The tawny owl's nictitating membranes are visible here.*

FRAMED

1700s

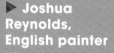

▶ **Joshua Reynolds, English painter**
Wore frames with extendable earpieces that fit under a wig.

early 1800s

▲ **Susan B. Anthony, American activist and suffragette**
Wore lightweight wire frames.

mid 1800s

▲ **Small and Portable**
A custom-fitted monocle was held in place by the eye muscles while in use.

late 1800s

Eyewear as style
Lorgnettes (glasses held with a handle) were stylish accessories.

early 1900s

20%
of children in the U.S. wear glasses.

THROUGH THE AGES

Nearly 2,000 years ago, Roman Emperor Nero held an emerald up to his eye to help him see gladiators compete. Some believed the emerald had a hole in it to help his eye focus or magnified the image. Others believed the green color helped shade the sun from his eyes. And during the Middle Ages (from the 5th to 15th century), people used polished reading stones.

Historians believe eyeglasses were invented in Italy between 1268 and 1289. They had heavy lenses made of quartz (a mineral found in rocks) that fit into bone or leather frames. In the 14th century, convex lenses to correct farsightedness were invented. Concave lenses to correct nearsightedness weren't invented until the 15th century. The invention of the printing press in 1452 led to an increased demand for reading glasses and eventually to changes in materials, styles, and availability.

Modern Styles

Serious, funky, or fun, eyeglasses make a style statement. What's next? Digital high-definition lenses, smart glasses with liquid lenses that adjust during use, and other advanced technologies may one day be as common as the eyeglass examples shown here.

KNOW A PRO: LASIK SURGEON

◀ **Theodore Roosevelt Jr., 26th U.S. president**
The pince-nez (meaning "pinch nose") style fit firmly on the nose to stay in place.

LASIK is a kind of eye surgery that uses a laser. It can correct nearsightedness and farsightedness in many people, depending on the kind of eye problems they have. Because eyes keep changing as children grow up, LASIK surgeons usually wait until someone is at least 18 years old to perform the surgery.

PEEPER PROBLEMS

If you are nearsighted or farsighted, prescription glasses can correct your vision. Other kinds of eye and vision problems may require treatment or special tools that can help.

▶ One Weak Eye

Amblyopia is a condition that occurs when the pathway between the eye and the brain doesn't develop properly. This may be because the eye is crossed, or because it does not focus properly. It usually affects only one eye, and is commonly called "lazy eye" because the affected eye does not work as well as the other one. Treatment may include special glasses to help strengthen the weaker eye, putting a patch on the better eye, and eye drops.

Glaucoma

High pressure inside the eye may cause damage to the optic nerve, which connects the eye to the brain. This is called glaucoma and is one of the leading causes of vision loss in older people. Eye doctors check for early evidence of glaucoma during regular check-ups. It can be treated with eye drops, medicine, or surgery.

◀ Cross-Eyes

When eyes don't line up or when one or both eyes wander, this is called strabismus. The eyes may turn inward or outward or up or down. This is because the brain and the muscles around the eyes aren't working together well. Treatments include eye exercises, eye patches, eye drops, eyeglasses, and sometimes eye muscle surgery.

▲ Pink and Itchy

Conjunctivitis, also called pink eye, is an infection in the lining under the eyelid (called the conjunctiva). Symptoms include swelling, itching or burning, and discharge (or goo). It is contagious and it is the most common eye problem that kids have. A doctor can determine whether treatment is needed.

READING BY TOUCH

Braille is a system of touch reading and writing. Letters and numbers are represented by raised dots. To read braille, a person moves their fingers across the dots from left to right along each line.

BRAILLE ALPHABET

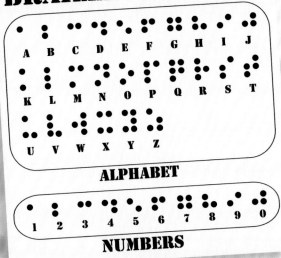

ALPHABET

NUMBERS

Helen Keller

Helen Keller was born in 1880. She was 19 months old when she lost her sight and hearing as a result of an illness called scarlet fever. Five years later, her parents applied for help to the Perkins Institute for the Blind. Anne Mansfield Sullivan was hired as Helen's teacher. Anne taught Helen everything about communicating with others, how to do things for herself, and how to read, write, and continue to learn.

Although Helen couldn't see or hear spoken words she learned to talk, write, read, and make friends. She went to college, wrote nearly a dozen books, traveled all over the world, met 12 U.S. presidents, and lived to be 87.

▶ Tap Tap Tap

A brailler is a braille typewriter. It has six dot-making keys that press dots into the page. Special machines give computers braille displays, too.

Electronic Braille Notetakers

These devices are small and portable. Students enter information on the braille keyboard and can transfer them later to a computer to store for future use.

Hear a Book

Audio books are ways to read with your ears. They are great ways to enjoy books for both vision-challenged and sighted people.

CAN YOU SEE IT NOW?

Optical illusions play tricks on our brains. They use color, light, shape, pattern, and perspective in ways that make it hard for us to figure out what we are seeing. Here are some examples of well-known optical illusions. Can you figure them out?

AMBIGUOUS FIGURE

Is that a doll house-size castle in a fountain? Look again. The fountain is in the foreground—very close—and the big castle is in the far distance. Because of the way it was taken, the photo makes it look like a miniature castle is sitting on the fountain.

CAFÉ WALL

How many curved rows do you see? The alternating positions of the black and white tiles make it look as though the rows are sloped down or up. If you focus on one horizontal row at a time, you'll see that they are all even and go straight across.

IMPOSSIBLE OBJECT

This two-dimensional picture looks like a 3D triangle to your brain. But the colored bars form parts of three different triangles, in a way that couldn't actually exist.

SPIN ILLUSION

It's a spinwheel! Color and pattern combine to make us think this image is spinning around. Experts say that tiny eye movements, combined with blinking, make our eyes see motion. These kinds of illusions make some people feel dizzy.

FIGURE-GROUND

This tree has a gnarly trunk! Now look at the white areas that form the background. Do you see two faces, one on either side of the tree?

OTHER THINGS WITH EYES

Here's a riddle: What has eyes but cannot see? Many things! Check out these "eyes" below.

The **eye of a needle** is the small oval opening that thread is looped through.

A **bull's-eye** is the center of an archery target or dart board. It's hard to hit and worth the most points.

The **eye of a hurricane** is the calm, quiet center of the storm.

A Brazilian frog with a long name has a pair of **false eyes** on its backside. The *Eupemphix nattereri* can inflate these false spots to make itself look large and fierce. The black centers produce a toxin strong enough to kill predators who dare take a bite.

Eyespots are markings found on some animals, including peacock tail feathers and owl butterfly wings.

EYE SAY

What does it mean if someone says, "Keep your eye on the ball?" Should you actually touch your eye to a ball? No! It means focus your attention on what you're doing. An expression that means something different from what it sounds like is called an idiom. Here are some eye idioms. See if you can guess what they mean. Then check below for definitions.

It's my birthday. I'm going to **keep an eye out** for packages in the mail.

1

If you can see that ship far offshore, you must have **eagle eyes**.

2

It seemed like a simple problem, but it took a long time to solve. There was **more than meets the eye**.

3

The pop quiz was a surprise, but I was cool— **I didn't bat an eyelid**.

4

From the top of the Ferris wheel, we had **a bird's-eye view** of the amusement park.

5

As soon as the rain stopped, a rainbow came out. It happened in the **blink of an eye**.

6

1. To watch carefully for something or someone due to arrive. 2. Like an eagle, to have amazing eyesight to spot things far away. 3. When there is something missing or hidden facts. 4. To not show any shock or surprise. 5. A broad view, as if from the sky like a bird. 6. A blink takes about 1/3 of a second, so this means very fast.

LIGHTS OUT

People have found ways to light up the dark for at least a million years (when the ability to create fire first appeared). Electric lighting has been around for 200 years and Thomas Edison's first light bulb was produced in 1879. Ever since, people have been inventing new ways to bring artificial light to places we go and things we do. Battery-powered flashlights have been around since 1899.

Electric light bulbs on **miner's hats** were first used in the early 1900s, bringing increased safety to workers. Before that, caps had oil or gas lamps, which could cause fires and explosions underground.

A **lighthouse** is a large tower with a bright light on the top called a beacon. The light inside the tower uses lamps and lenses to create a guide for boats so they can avoid reefs and find safe harbors. It can shine up to 25 miles out to sea.

Sunlight can reach a few hundred feet below the ocean surface, but it doesn't provide enough light for a curious scuba diver. A waterproof **dive light** helps light the way as a diver explores a busy coral reef.

Glow sticks are fun for Halloween, parties, and campouts. They contain two chemicals that release energy when combined by bending the plastic light stick. This energy creates light.

Flashlights create a beam of light that helps us see in the dark. Headlamp flashlights are good for reading and exploring.

Camping lanterns light up a tent after dark for backyard and nature campouts. Be sure to pack extra batteries, so the light doesn't go out in the middle of a scary ghost story!

FARANDAWAY

The moon is 238,855 miles away and sunlight travels 93 million miles to warm our planet. There's a lot to see in our solar system and beyond, and special tools that help us get a closer look.

STAR GAZING

Telescopes collect light and magnify an image to make it look larger. There are two different kinds.

Refracting telescopes use lenses that bend light to collect it and focus an image.

Reflecting telescopes use mirrors and lenses to collect light to focus an image. These telescopes create a clearer picture than refracting telescopes.

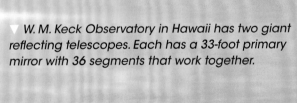

STAR MAP Polaris has been helping people find their way for centuries. It is in the sky above the North Pole, and is often called the North Star. So if you face Polaris, you are facing north.

▼ W. M. Keck Observatory in Hawaii has two giant reflecting telescopes. Each has a 33-foot primary mirror with 36 segments that work together.

COSMIC LIGHTHOUSES

Pulsars are among the brightest objects in space. They are formed when stars explode. They spin so fast that their light appears to flicker. Like a lighthouse lamp, they have a steady blinking rhythm.

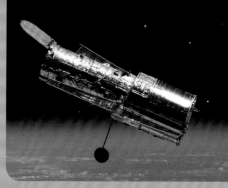

OUT OF SIGHT The Hubble Space Telescope was launched on April 24, 1990, to explore space and send images to scientists on Earth. It has made more than 1 million discoveries since then. Here are just a few.

ASTRONAUT VISION

In space, fluid in the body moves upward and this puts added pressure on the eyes. Over time, this can make the back of the eyeball flat, irritate the optic nerve, and make it hard to see close up or far away. Experts are studying astronauts while they live on the International Space Station and when they return to find ways to prevent these vision issues.

▲ Astronaut Karen Nyberg performs an eye exam on the International Space Station.

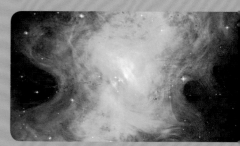

Ghost Light After a star dies, its light continues to glow.

Starring Role This bright star outshines the rest of its constellation, Lacerta (the Lizard).

◄ A laser helps guide the Keck telescope observations.

Spot This Jupiter's Great Red Spot is a gigantic storm twice as wide as Earth.

43

RESOURCES

MUSEUMS

Museum of Vision
American Academy of Ophthalmology
San Francisco, CA
The Museum of Vision is the only museum
dedicated to the science of vision. It has
over 38,000 artifacts that show the history of
ophthalmology. They have kid-friendly activities
such as optical illusions, an animal eyes exhibit,
and an art and vision series.

ZOO WEBSITES

Learn about animals, watch them on video
cameras, and play games at the San Diego Zoo
online: **kids.sandiegozoo.org**

At the Smithsonian's National Zoo site, meet the
animals that live there and watch the giant pandas,
elephants, and lions on webcams: **nationalzoo.
si.edu/animals**

BOOKS

Eye to Eye: How Animals See the World
By Steve Jenkins
If you're wondering how animals see the world and
how their eyes have evolved, read this book.

Animal Eyes
By Dona Herweck Rice
This book explores the variation of
eyes in the animal kingdom.

MUSEUM WEBSITES

For more information on how to keep your eyes healthy, how they work, and much more about the eyes and other parts of your body, click on How the Body Works at: *kidshealth.org*

The American Foundation for the Blind, founded in 1921, is dedicated to expanding the possibilities for people with vision loss. Visit *afb.org* for more information, and check out their child-focused site: *braillebug.afb.org*

The Braille Institute organizes an annual skills and mobility competition for blind and visually impaired students grades 3–12 called Cane Quest. To learn more, visit: *brailleinstitute.org*

To learn more about Buddy, the first seeing eye dog in the United States, visit: *seeingeye.org*

To see information and videos on how to keep your eyes healthy, how they work, and much more, check out: *kidshealth.org/en/kids/eyes-movie.html?WT.ac=en-k-htbw-main-page-b*

To learn more about animal eyes, and things that look like eyes, but aren't, check out: *saczoo.org/2015/10/the-eyes-have-it*

To learn more about the anatomy of the eye, including diagrams, check out: *livescience.com/3919-human-eye-works.html*

This eye foundation website has more information about diseases of the eye and their symptoms: *discoveryeye.org*

SELECTED SOURCES
Many sources were used in gathering facts about eyes and vision. Here are some of them.

Guide Animals: The Guide Horse Foundation; The Seeing Eye Dog Foundation. **Eyes and Eye Health:** American Academy of Pediatrics; National Eye Institute; American Optometric Association. **Other:** BBC Earth; National Public Radio; Discover Magazine.

ACKNOWLEDGMENTS

From the author:
Thank you to Miss Stacey Webb's kindergarten class at Brown's Valley Elementary School in Vacaville, California who provided honest feedback and helped make this book fun! Thank you to Amy Barry, Ethan Wang and David Wolfington for assisting in research for this book.

From Scout Books & Media:
We would like to express our gratitude to the talented team at Seagrass Press and Quarto, including Josalyn Moran, Shelley Baugh, and April Balotro-Carothers. With special thanks to Michael S. Rentz, PhD, Lecturer in Mammalogy at Iowa State University, for his invaluable guidance on animals and their eyes, for boundless enthusiasm in sharing his knowledge with others, and to Dr. Maury Marmor, ophthalmologist and professor who specializes in pediatric ophthalmology and strabismus, for his contributions on eyes and vision, and how best to take care of our eyes.

GLOSSARY

bifocals Glasses or lenses with two sections. Bifocals allow the wearer see close up and far away by looking at different parts of the lens.

binocular vision Two eyes working together to produce a single image. This helps with judging distances.

bioluminescence Light produced by a living animal through a chemical process in its body.

compound eye An eye that has many light-sensing elements. Most insects have compound eyes.

dilate To expand or make larger. Pupils dilate in dim light.

eyespot A light-sensitive spot on the body of an invertebrate animal, or a rounded eyelike marking on an animal.

farsighted Being able to see better farther away and less well close up.

genes Genes carry information that determines the characteristics from your parents that are passed on to you.

heterochromia Having eyes that are two different colors.

infection An illness that is caused by bacteria or viruses.

invertebrate An animal without a backbone.

invisible light Light that can't be seen by the human eye.

LASIK Eye surgery that uses a laser.

melanin A pigment in the body that affects the color of the eyes, hair, and skin.

membrane A thin layer of tissue that covers, lines, or connects parts of the body.

monocular vision Two eyes, usually on either side of the head, that can see independently of each other. Animals with monocular vision can see two different things at once.

nearsighted Being able to see better close up and less well farther away.

nocturnal Happening at night. Bats are nocturnal—they sleep during the day and are active at night.

optic nerve A nerve that sends information from the retina of the eye to the brain.

optical illusion When an image or object tricks the eye by appearing to be something it is not.

predator An animal that hunts and eats other animals.

prey An animal that is hunted and eaten by other animals.

refraction When a ray of light is bent by a lens or a drop of water. Eyes and cameras use refraction to record images.

simple eye An eye with one lens.

ultraviolet light A type of light that the human eye can't see. Also called UV light, its presence in sunlight causes suntans and sunburns.

vertebrate An animal with a backbone.

visible light Light the human eye can see.

wavelength The distance between one wave of light or sound and the next one. Different colors have different wavelengths.

INDEX

Illustrations are indicated by **boldface**. When illustrations fall within a page span, the entire span of pages is **boldface**.

PHOTO CREDITS

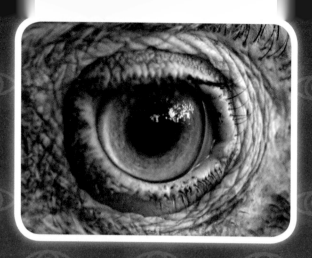

1 The eyeball! Ostriches have the largest eyes of all land animals.

2 An octopus can rotate its pupils so that they're always horizontal, even when the animal is swimming sideways.

3 Yes, their eyes have clear membranes that work like goggles to protect them.

LEXILE LEVEL:
A.R. POINTS:
A.R. LEVEL: